An Alphabet of Last Rites

Marc Vincenz

Červená Barva Press
West Somerville, Massachusetts

Červená Barva Press
P.O. Box 440357
W. Somerville, MA 02144-3222

www.cervenabarvapress.com

Bookstore: www.thelostbookshelf.com

ISBN: 978-1-950063-94-9

Cover Image: *Birch Grove* by Arkhip Kuindzhi, 1879

An Alphabet of Last Rites

A.

The fingers, the soft fingers, almost transparent, abandoned, but not cold. A burst, a flurry, a flutter, not unlike any lukewarm harvest you might feed me.

B.

The hair in curls and folds. That curlicue on your forehead like some 20s flapper dancer. How the curl returns after all these years; and the rice on your chin, all the Chinese you ever wished for—*Gong Hei Fat Choy*, Sweet Fingers. *You* were all I could have ever wished for; it curls and folds and doubles up, and it flies away: the distant cries of the lone crow crossing the cloudbank.

C.

A word in your ear, please. If all we ever found here were fool's gold—but for heaven's sake, get dressed; we can't have people seeing you like that—we might think ourselves clever; the eyes are dizzied by some unseen fortune. The starling lifts a silver ring with a 24-carat diamond and thinks it's a hard nut.

D.

And in the folds and creases much is ironed out, no doubt
all those creams you applied in your lifetime, and the
ointments and the multivitamins and the extra collagen
and calcium; the cabbage eaten every Sunday, the right light
three times of day. When the moon was full, you said one
hour would give you years of wrinkle-free skin. It worked.

E.

The country we're supposed to be headed for is rich in mineral resources and cheap labor. The country we're coming from is rich in the middle where all the girth accumulates. It hits you in the teeth when you walk out the door. Never forget, though, the last words are inevitably the second go-to.

F.

Always with the neck extended, as if the last leaf were always the best.

A long road rambles within us.

G.

An extended metaphor like the one I'm using now has to
have teeth and flesh. The tiger pacing the millionaire's pool
in Bangladesh, for example; and the blood in her whiskers,
a sneak-peak of early evenings in your swimsuit, martini in
hand; your hair wrapped up in a towel turban; and later,
the obligatory kaftan, the silver pumps that once belonged
to Eva Peron.

"Anyone can be an actress," you once said, "but few have
become a dictator."

H.

Eva Peron? Josephine Bonaparte? Catherine the Great? Queen Elizabeth I, Marie Antoinette? Madame Curie? Queen Victoria? Who was it that said, "We are not amused"?

1.

In a hundred years of poetry, how many lives have been saved? You were always the one on the front lines. I can tell you what she with the halo said. She said: "The image took hold. The world does not forget the bold. He became what people pictured him to be."

J.

All these beliefs based on reality. Surely it's more important to have faith in the characters. While each second passes, souls arise and go. That's what the sun is for.

K.

All the lights and mirrors, the mannequins and the racks of costumes and masks, all the feathers. And the feather-dusters.

"The extraterrestrials have taken off. Actually, they're just at the bar down the road. You tell me. Is this something I should be afraid of?"

L.

Whatever she writes, she writes for life. A person can believe anything, especially kinfolk. She knew her worth on most markets. So much for life, eh?

M.

Emboldened, empathetic, empowered, emphatic.

Love on the misty lake.

N.

An announcement of sorts:

So derelict. Through the window all sorts of catastrophes. Even sitting on the sunny porch like someone ready for a journey when a lunatic cyclist crosses your way; even after the homemade bread and the homemade wine, the wind soaks up your sweat with those passing ghosts.

Another good reason to trust in ancient gods, another reason for all the adoration paid to the sun, another reason for nailing a man to the cross, and yet another reason to peel off all those profanities and other inclement measures, all facing an indeterminate address, the ultimate success fading ... fading out.

M².

Again, another spin around the block. You can spin a hundred times, but you know eventually you've got to stop. And when you stop, there are thieves, pirates, dastardly characters you've only seen on the silver screen.

Enter stage left, a man with a sword.

In a word, in retort to your repartee, from all you've ever been caught; the labyrinth, the Minotaur, the headless beast who bumps along the walls of the inner chamber.

Out of sight, in a word.

O.

As in open or opened, released, set forth. An agent of the scarcely proficient, a matter-abuser, a bad crop, a lonely money-guy, another hundred centuries deep, past the stoplights; the reason for treason in the deepest of tracks, the score of Scorsese in the woods, the De Niro in deliverance, the Pacino on acceptance; later, the Frodo Elijah Wood.

Somewhere there is a pawn of blemished, bleached skin who breathes the conditional hollows, who follows the snow like a burr caught on fur, like all those who have gone before, or in addendum, in annexium, like the rexium in all his splendor, the boy on the throne in the know more that you know.

P.

Walking through the marshlands in the old country, sounding out the runaway geese but all I hear is the hoot of the barn owl even though it's early afternoon. Has she been up all night?

You can clearly see the landing strips of the geese that left and somehow you can still hear their voices on the air. An ornithologist friend once told me she mis-tagged half a dozen of them and they ended up somewhere on the Aran Isles, a million miles from where they should have landed. I wonder how many have wedded here among the brambles along the shoreside as I wade home to an empty home.

Q.

A seventh symphony bustles in my head, buzzes in my inner ear; something like the sound of you while we were stumbling in your veins and structures. It's microbial almost, and just like its host, it thrives on soft cheeses.

There's no need to pretend we could grasp any of this.

R.

The second time you were arrested, you looked like a decaying birch tree trying to hang on to its shadow. It took you months to find birds willing to perch on your limbs—even a quick peck—in much the same way it took me months to master basic French.

"Pardon my French," you said.

S.

And here we have the essence of it:

Five drams of formaldehyde to two of malt whiskey, a shot
of Drambuie, a flake of chili pepper, a stake in at the races,
a fly or two in your ear.

When you're done, know it's not the size of the pot; mostly
it's the way it's stirred. And when you strain the essence,
concentrate the masses in a faint swirl.

T.

As jazz has been said to cool limbs, like a shot of bourbon, so the blues construes the racing heart in advance. In the same vein, Allan Quatermain set out across the Gobi Desert and encountered not one, but two sets of high-profilers: an ancient Illurian emperor and a Newt King embalmed astride a stone throne.

Q².

In line with the Caliphate, we follow house rules, everything and everyone duly noted.

The war is over. Since when is rightful vengeance a sin? it has been written.

There was an old man who lived once on the banks of the Tiber who in all his sorcery saw fit to turn rice to flour and flour to flatbread.

Watch for those windmills that grind essential elements into one big paste.

R².

Hovering by my curtains to my surprise
A small creature appears. He's small.
He has warts on his nose. He says:
"Is this all you do, Squire?"
I say: "Is this the way you treat a lady?"
He says: "Pardon my manners, Madame. And,
By the way, aren't you lovely, Madame."
"Mixed dialects," I say, tapping the side of my head.

S².

Sodium sulfate to make your clear white paper.

Are those the same old stories?

T².

Me too, like a herring schooling around.

U.

Alone again. The daughter of a lighthouse keeper, evening after evening, sending out signals; then maybe a cigarette before bed overlooking the cool, dark ocean. All night the waves lap at her shores.

In your dreams you wade through a marsh of razors.

It seems someone wants to keep you just to throw you away. This in her words (my words too, if I'm honest): "Just how many times did they announce it on the megaphone?"

Yes, you're running late again. May I commiserate with you on what has not been stolen?

This strange creature has something to hide.

V.

Distressing all these elements.

Generations of memory written on a cell, and we, like distant godchildren playing in the sand.

If you like, emptiness lies between your legs. Just like the crab or the turtle, on these days, the surf is ripe.

Don't get too close. She has a knife in her hand.

Don't we want peace right now whilst we're still among the living? I could have written this story one thousand times, but something held me back. I didn't want to tell it in the third person or have it told behind my back, whispered in coffeeshops and bistros along the Avenue Centrale among the mannequins and tumbling clowns.

There is this non-divine state as you lean over a rose; a measurement of things, if you will, where—how do I tell you this?—the only ending is the final ending.

DOUBLE U.

Why not.

X.

Hallowed ground. Skirting along the borders in a green shimmer with a handful of square stones engraved in such words as: The wife of somesuch died here, or the daughter without a name who lived longer than most, or even, after this there is nothing more …

But I ask you: what is the definition of nothing? Surely we're all compacted in a hole of our own making.

Watch the ducks floating on the pond.

Do you hear their prayer?

X².

And yet, for a little hopeful measure, your lips, when you swing through a hole in the sky; your eyelids, when you flutter them; you bet we're all sand-banked, stranded; it's as if you see through objects; forget all the infinite tales of the divine acrobats, of stars in their sunken façades, of fresh fruit or another reason to live; forget all these things, and let's move stealthily toward the reeds.

X³.

And for all of you others who snuggle up against stainless steel piping or the geothermal miracle of the heart at the center of the world, of the blood that flows around the earth at every single minute. "Small things," as my mother would say over her fourth martini in the old days when there was still a connection.

Y.

"Why all this becoming rather than being?" she said.

"Blame Darwin," I said, playing with the fuzz on the back of my arm.

"There are longings and then there are long-ings," I said.

She said, "You think you have all this figured out." And at that moment, she was right. I did. A second later, the sky broke and something hard hit my head.

When I awoke, she said, "You do so ramble on." And, "Still, you have a way with words."

I swear it wasn't going to my head.

"Show me yours if I show you mine," she said.

z.

The last in a long line of healers, and a true believer all the way down to your apple core. Of course you swallowed them all and swore on them. Who could blame you.

You'll need to be like this when you leave your life. When the time comes, keep all your secrets tucked in your sleeves and pockets, and in that bundle of hair stacked high like a Great Bake cake.

There are times when I wish I knew the art of icing.

The Author

www.ingramcontent.com/pod-product-compliance
Lightning Source LLC
Chambersburg PA
CBHW021348060726
47591CB00006B/2220